ETERNITY SHIMMERS
TIME HOLDS ITS BREATH

other books by the author

POETRY
Dawn Visions
Burnt Heart/Ode to the War Dead
This Body of Black Light Gone Through the Diamond
The Desert is the Only Way Out
The Chronicles of Akhira
The Blind Beekeeper
Mars & Beyond
Laughing Buddha Weeping Sufi
Salt Prayers
Ramadan Sonnets
Psalms for the Brokenhearted
I Imagine a Lion
Coattails of the Saint
Abdallah Jones and the Disappearing-Dust Caper (illustrated by the author)
Love is a Letter Burning in a High Wind
The Flame of Transformation Turns to Light
Underwater Galaxies
The Music Space
Cooked Oranges
Through Rose Colored Glasses
Like When You Wave at a Train and the Train Hoots Back at You
In the Realm of Neither
The Fire Eater's Lunchbreak
Millennial Prognostications
You Open a Door and it's a Starry Night
Where Death Goes
Shaking the Quicksilver Pool
The Perfect Orchestra
Sparrow on the Prophet's Tomb
A Maddening Disregard for the Passage of Time
Stretched Out on Amethysts
Invention of the Wheel
Sparks Off the Main Strike
Chants for the Beauty Feast
In Constant Incandescence
Holiday from the Perfect Crime
The Caged Bear Spies the Angel
The Puzzle
Ramadan is Burnished Sunlight
Ala-udeen & The Magic Lamp (illustrated by the author)
The Crown of Creation (illustrated by the author)
Blood Songs
Down at the Deep End (with drawings by the author)
Next Life
A Hundred Little 3D Pictures
He Comes Running (chapbook)
Miracle Songs for the Millennium
Some
The Throne Perpendicular to All that is Horizontal
The Soul's Home
Eternity Shimmers / Time Holds its Breath

THEATER / THE FLOATING LOTUS MAGIC OPERA COMPANY
The Walls Are Running Blood
Bliss Apocalypse

ETERNITY SHIMMERS
TIME HOLDS ITS BREATH

poems

Ocober 10, 2013 – January 27, 2014

●

Daniel Abdal-Hayy Moore

The Ecstatic Exchange
2014
Philadelphia

Eternity Shimmers / Time Holds its Breath
Copyright © 2014 Daniel Abdal-Hayy Moore
All rights reserved.
Printed in the United States of America

For quotes any longer than those for critical articles and reviews, contact:
The Ecstatic Exchange,
6470 Morris Park Road, Philadelphia, PA 19151-2403
email: abdalhayy@danielmoorepoetry.com

First Edition
ISBN: 978-0-578-14810-6 (paper)
Published by *The Ecstatic Exchange*,
6470 Morris Park Road, Philadelphia, PA 19151-2403

(Note: The poem sequence of *He Comes Running* is also available in a separate 4X6 inch chapbook format, with calligraphic designs by Haji Noor Deen Mi Guang Jiang, available on Amazon.com, Lulu.com and directly from the author.)

Front cover art by Malika Moore, *The Rainbow Bismin*, based on the famous calligraphy by Moroccan Shaykh Muhammad b. Al-Qasim al-Qandusi (died:1861)

Back cover photograph © Lou Wilson

 بس

DEDICATION
To
Shaykh ibn al-Habib
(and the continuation of the Habibiyya)
Shaykh Bawa Muhaiyuddeen,
all shuyukh of instruction and ma'arifa ,
wife Malika, my bond and solace,
family near and far
on whose waves of prayer I am buoyed
by Allah,
Dr. Peter Prociuk, Healer,
and
Baji Tayyaba Khanum
of the unsounded depths

The earth is not bereft
of Light

CONTENTS

ETERNITY SHIMMERS

Watching a Cat Drink Water   10
Take a Bottle for Example   11
If a Centipede   13
If a Beam of Light   15
A Little House   16
Scritch Scratch   18
Any Hippopotamus   20
Whenever Has God's Radiance   22
I Wonder   23
A Giant Stood Up   25
Miracle Inspection   27
Black Horse   30
Prayer   31
Car Sticker   32
An Elegy to Loss   33
The Things   35
Did You Know?   36
The Mournful Dog   39
Motionless Flashes in the Air   41
A Drunk Kept Knocking   43
The Scent of the Lord   46
His Voice   51
Everything is Auto-Suggestion   52

HE COMES RUNNING

Introduction   56
He Comes Running   59
Myths We Never Knew   98

TIME HOLDS ITS BREATH

Eternity   106
Cap and Bells   110
Time Holds its Breath   111
The UniverSoul Circus   113
The Rowers All Row   117
Don't Turn Away Just Yet   119
Our Hearts are Gongs   121
Everything That Can Be Said   122
The Serpent That Sizzles   124
Eating Stars   127
If We Put a Thousand Bridges   129
There's Nothing to be Done   132
Well of Blue Water   134
Your Whole Face   136
Sitting on Top of the Planet   138
Sphere of Light   140
Joy in God's World   142
If We Could Step Inside   144
The Curse of a Moment   146
Wings of Oblivion   148
Sitting With a Saint   151
New Boots   153
Deep Foreverland   155
I Awaken Each Day   157
He Waits by the Gate   158
With the Sensibility of Gyroscopes   160
Twig-Like Bird Prints   163
Nigerian Song Bird   165
He Comes Running   166

INDEX   168

"The people of heaven see the houses on earth in which the name of Allah the Exalted is remembered as you see stars in the sky"
— Narrated by Abu Hurayra (*may Allah be pleased with him*)

ETERNITY SHIMMERS

WATCHING A CAT DRINK WATER

As long as it takes a
cat to drink

is just about as long as
we'll live this life

at the brink of the edge
we'll soon fall off

into a sky so blue
a landing so soft

wings aren't needed
to fly to safety

as tiny as a bird's body
gets us safely

there in God's air
ajar in every place

for us to fly through
His open space

10/10

TAKE A BOTTLE FOR EXAMPLE

Take a bottle for example

It has a mouth
and can contain anything we

put in it

Can it contain a chair?
It can contain a

ship if you know how to
do it

Can it contain a house
with all its

windows and doors?

Can we contain all this
world with all its

windows and doors?

Even if we
know how to do it?

How do we do it?
By letting it all in?

Rats and alligators
tyrants and injustices?

But the miracle is
God says *"The*

world cannot contain Me

*but the believer's heart
contains Me"*

If we pour the bottle out
and look at the

world through its
curved glass

and change the glass
to God's Names

and the Great Name
surrounding all

then the world cannot
contain us

but our hearts can
contain God

10/13

IF A CENTIPEDE

If a centipede wore shoes
would he make more noise

walking on a leaf?

If birds wore saddles could they give
grasshoppers rides?

Would mice prefer their cheese on
little crackers and a pot of tea?

If all the world were as round as we
think it is would we all

rush together in loving solidarity?

Or is it as flat as it seems to us and we
walk miles for a friendly hug or

handshake and invitation inside a
Bedouin's tent?

God's radiance falls equally on
everyone and everything

and equally from within us all at
exactly the same rate and at

precisely always o'clock

It's the reason we can recognize a
wink and a nod across races

generations and even species if we
pay attention gently enough

— an owl looking at us suddenly
or a curious deer —

I can't get this gorgeousness
out of my system Lord

since You've put it there for
all to enjoy in this

swift blink toward Paradise

10/14

IF A BEAM OF LIGHT

If a beam of light is traveling along a
windowsill because the

earth is rotating
(fascinating the cat or even we might take

time to actually follow its course)
but then it comes to the frame and

disappears
has it gone back to the Source

dancing among the fiery explosions of the
sun or maybe now simply

traveling along the outside of the house?

Or has it ever really left its source
but rather stays with its source while it

leaps its entire length from the sun and
moves across our windowsill for our

edification and amusement
or feline amazement

that light can go so far and still be
one with its origin?

10/15

A LITTLE HOUSE

A little house on the edge of a leaf
and a hermit lives inside

enjoying sunrises and sunsets
and sweeping his front step —

a sweeping that is never done

He was asked by a passing dragonfly
the reason for his happiness

so he sat back a bit with his
hand at his chin

and said in a voice no louder than a
bee's while it's massaging the

longevity of plants and flowers
and painting the spring every bit of

gold it has slickered down its
stems and stamens

The hermit leaned back looking
out into the sky and said

"If God isn't here with us right now
then where is He?

On His ranch in some dusty heaven?
Out in mid-ocean urging the

ocean waves on? Out in mid-space
smoothing the orbital highways for their

respective planets?

He's here right now
making us happy

unless we insist on being sad
both to ourselves and others

until owls fall from their trees
and crickets go silent?"

10/16

SCRITCH SCRATCH

for Khaliff Watkins

Scritch scratch
a mouse behind the wainscoting

Scritch scratch
clouds scraping past each other in sunlight

Scritch scratch
writing in streaks of wind on the

way to God

No end to the scritching and the
scratching of a giraffe's vertebrae

as it stretches its neck to the top leaves
the most scrumptious of the tree

No end to us all
scritching and scratching our hearts out

by lamplight past midnight or on
bus ride alone from Chinatown to Miami

all the world whooshing past the window
as we flee from one space to a

future one only a few seconds ahead

Scritching and scratching words on
paper from words moving their

blue and orange lips in our hearts

like mice behind walls
and ice-pebble satellites in

Saturn's rings maybe not making actual
scritch scratch sounds but

high-pitched singing like tea kettles as they
whistle around like

birds freed from their cages
singing only for God in their

ever new-found freedom their
wings beating wordless

scritch-scratch phrases
in the sky

10/19

ANY HIPPOPOTAMUS

"Any hippopotamus could tell you
what it's like to be a

hippopotamus

but only humans of all the species can
pretend to know what it's

like to be a hippo to the yawning of the
mouth and coming up out of

water with dainty waterlily doilies
dripping on our heads

Not that there aren't many instances of
animal imitation such as the

menacing faces made from
dark spots on certain Amazonian

butterfly wings

or one animal imitating the screams and
chittering sounds of another

Elephants are the only
mammals that can't jump

and humans the only
mammals that can put on

complete Broadway musicals in
outlandish sparkling cat costumes

and this gives us certain
responsibilities that we

shirk at our peril"

he said before
turning back to sleep

                10/19

WHENEVER HAS GOD'S RADIANCE

Whenever has God's radiance failed?

Antelopes leap and
lions roar?

Over what mountaintops eagles scream
and in what valleys

long green rivers flow?

What heartbeats missing on this
rocky planet?

What wave missing from the
Seven Seas?

What breath missing from our
godly allotment

that small birds fly inside
on their way to night?

If we hold out our hearts under God's
waterfall

it forms a cup for more than it can
bear

and passes it around
and passes it around

I WONDER

I wonder if when we leave this world
we'll turn a page and find it was

made entirely of silver and straw

and all the twilights and brilliance
cat hair and sweet cat faces gazing

deep into our eyes from their
animal pupils

worlds upon worlds and worlds
wrapped within worlds of

bewildering complexity were really only
the concave reflection of silvery

light and light-as-straw
realities in domed skies of holy

Remembrance
all of it

No shred of our lives anything
more or less than this

gorgeousness and excitement the
memorization of angels

layered choirs of our heartbeats each
one of which

steps closer to God's Infinite
Intimacy

the other side
(as well as this side)

of the page we
turn

when we die

                                                             10/24

A GIANT STOOD UP

A giant stood up one day
his head reaching the clouds

and he was shocked to find
someone standing on his shoulders

and craning his head a little
saw someone on that one's

shoulders and folk all the way
up to where he couldn't see

anything at all

"Who are you?" he bellowed
and the vibration shivered all the way

up to the topmost whomever
for this was one formidable giant

"We're the future generations indebted to you sir"
yelled down in strange harmony all the

ones standing on the last one's shoulders

*"and without you sir we'd be
nothing!"*

The giant managed to lean down and
break off a piece of mirror

(he was standing in his outside grotto)
and angled it just so to see up the

line as far as he could
and how at the very top

they disappear into light

He's still standing there for
each one of us for

one reason or another even if it's
just simple genetics which

really isn't all that simple

and if you stand in your grotto in a
certain light you might see the

folk in the unseen who for
some reason or other

are standing on your
shoulders

all the way up
into the light

10/24

MIRACLE INSPECTION

Each miracle lines up to be inspected

Some are hard to contain
others are always in mid-manifestation

and finding adequate space for some
can be problematic

since space itself is one of them

The trees that give off fruit are
lining up on all the sky lanes

Rivers whose pure waters always
sparkle as they thrill over stones

Pathways through forests and
jungles stand next to each other

as tight as possible and they
still spill over and barely fit together

Light and darkness have to take
turns as each seems to

supersede the other
so they work out a kind of

flickering with just a nanosecond enough
for a proper inspection to take place

and we haven't even mentioned air
and where it goes

nor life itself that has to be
experienced to be believed

that stands for a moment as
still as possible and puts on its

best face before having to go
back to being in continuous and

tumultuous motion

and then the death of all this is
called on for inspection

and has to find a place to slide in
almost undistinguished and

not in a way that jeopardizes all the
others although its ubiquity is

noticeable and spontaneity
taken note of

in the cosmic scheme of things

The cosmic scheme of things is also
inspected there where it

flourishes pulling out its
shoots and flowers galaxies and

stars and its delirious
musical perfumes that intoxicate each

miraculous living creature of us
as we also go to the inspection ground

in the midst of all this
and pray to pass along with

everything else to earn
a noble and

beloved reward

                                                           10/25

BLACK HORSE

As sleek and fine a black horse
as you'd expect to find on a

horse farm in the highlands

as fierce in its being who it is as
the air in which it walks and

holds its head just so with
any number of cloud shapes changing

above it or mountain ranges behind it
as it gallops along the shore in

sea glisten and sky shine riderless as
it is its own horseman and only

God knows who other than it could
be its rider other than

Himself in all its perfect nature
other than Himself in fact

in all its perfect nature

PRAYER

Let me see You in all things today

The sheer perfectness of You

                                                        10/26

CAR STICKER

On the back of the car in front of me
a sticker said in big letters:

"Wagging more"

and below it in small letters:

"and barking less."

10/26

AN ELEGY TO LOSS

I can't even remember most of the
things I've lost

A particular photograph that
struck a gong in my heart and could

never be lost

Things of inestimable value that for a
few days occupied my mind in that

great washing machine of thinly
sloshing thoughts

leaving it and coming back to it or it
leaving me and coming back again like

dental floss that you thought you dropped
into the waste basket but is

still on your finger

but much thinner really and
evanescent even than that metaphor

And then people lost that should
never have been lost

and not lost really but the onward moving
cloud of time and space surrounded them

heartbeat after heartbeat in its
passing

and took them with it and
you felt their loss and wondered if they

felt yours at all in their ongoing sunlit space

All lost

Forever lost
all these oceans of things that at

low tide go way out and you find
you're on dry land in some sweet space

surrounded by nothing but
loss

10/28

THE THINGS

The things of this world
are less than you expected

The things of the next world
are more than you imagined

                                                       10/28

DID YOU KNOW?

Did you know that the
Great Pyramid at Giza moves a few inches

east each year and that one day it might
sit right next to the Nile?

That the Grand Canyon closes its great
wound a few inches each decade and that

one day it could again be a smooth
and contiguous earth-flats?

That the orbit of Pluto that at some point
disqualified it from planetary status

actually makes a Mobius strip loop
going around back the way it came?

Of course none of these things are
true

I just finished reading that
"There is no pure physics

*but always the physics of some
definite psychic activity"*

by Henri Corbin who wrote extensively about
Shaykh Ibn al 'Arabi

That every world seen by everyone in the world
is a collective personal vision of it

transparently overlapping from the unique
unity of our human

divinely given consciousness somehow
fixing if only for a moment or

continuous flickering of moments a
somewhat stable picture of the

universe we find ourselves in

with all its erratic and
occasionally peaceful behavior

wars turning into
sitting down together and having

tea and sitting down together having tea
turning into bonobo monkey eruptions

How God's luminous landscapes dance in our
eyes and how our hearts

actualize God's Divine Names in gore and
in glory

that pure hearts register
light out of darkness

and impure hearts
darkness out of light

                                        10/30 (over Normandy)

THE MOURNFUL DOG

for Lou Wilson

The mournful dog a mile away
knows a thing or two

and the colossal amount of space above
the Bosphorus at night when

freighters plow its waters knows secrets

The slightest sparrow in that flock
that spotted itself in the

sparse linden tree then whirringly dispersed

outside the Blue Mosque has a
secret in its heart

The golden rays of light from the
cloud-cut opening at their

divine angle even they from
where they came and where as they

hit the strait below they were
going know a high altitude secret

as do all such golden
rays

and may we also speed to that

place conscious of His Light
each carrying the inestimable

secrets from before birth to the
decreed Land of Secrets revealed

beyond this life
as night edges minute by minute

toward dawn

                                                              11/1 (Istanbul)

MOTIONLESS FLASHES IN THE AIR

The leader of the wolf pack
drew back his lips and snarled

His teeth gleamed in the moonlight

The melting snowman took on a
truly malevolent look as it

slid into slush

Windows in an abandoned building
gave it a haunted glower at the

same point each sunset

Why does God mask His manifestations
in sometimes dark sometimes light

faces?

War cuts through countries like
burnt tire tread of a giant

monster six-wheel

People often frighten themselves
to death

In hospitals illness takes on a
Frankenstein aspect with all its tubes and

beeps

whereas we know death's a sweet
grasshopper under a leaf

taking its shade

and a feather slowly twisting as it
falls delicately through the air

But things have to go as they're meant to
and the wolves' teeth flash so and

smoking cities reek so
only as disguises for a

beauty too fiery to bear
but Allah's Face remains benign

as everything else moves in motionless
flashes in the air

11/2

A DRUNK KEPT KNOCKING

A drunk kept knocking on the same door
until a hand came out

and dragged him in

It was nowhere you can imagine
and everywhere you can see

Its presence lasts as long as your love
lets it and gets it and knows

it's there behind every appearance
and the reality of every appearance

*"He is the Outwardly Manifest
and the Inwardly Hidden"*

The drunk never knew what hit him
when the ceiling became the floor

and the floor the sky so filled with
flocks of tropical sweet-singing birds

the sun had to sing even louder than
usual to shine through

And this was just the first moments of
his endless rapture to come

because such a gulp of the innermost
air never left him from that moment

even if circumstances changed and seemed to
go back to "normal"

The owl that sang in a nearby tree
threw sagacious glances at his heart

Ripples in the sea kept an enchanting
syncopation from then on he could

feel in the pulse in his wrist

"Be drunk" he'd say to those bland
passersby whose blank stares didn't

become them
and he knew that only that echoing tavern

would truly become them

and each passing tree and each roving
breeze thenceforward

knew of him and threw shade on his
passing and cooled his righteous passage

for he knew Who owned the tavern and how He
now watched over him with

ever-increasing compassionate concern
and his road thenceforward

though crooked as before and covered in
brambles the way the Prophet's was

took him to that same door
at which he knocked

and each time at that same door
he knocked at

a hand dragged him in
as before

11/4

THE SCENT OF THE LORD

1

As the distinct scent of coffee that
like a sword cuts its

way through the air to our nostrils
and if we follow it to its source

soon we'll be sitting in front of a
frothy cup of that delicious brew

so O Lord let us follow the scent of You
the news of You the cried tears and sudden

shouts of You on high seas and dry land
that through the air everywhere

even beyond geographies and nationalities
like that pure awakening scent of

coffee opens our senses and our thirst
to put all aside and make our

way past every obstruction to get to You
knowing by it You're here and then knowing

that in fact the very You of You is both
nowhere at all and everywhere at once

overpowering in Your Presence and making
all other scents and unrealities

of no consequence

2

There's a dog down the road that
won't stop barking

a moon that won't stop shining

a world that won't stop
dissolving away

and You Lord a diamond light that
won't cease attracting us to Your

rare shine its facets that reflect
every gleam possible in each desperate

moment facet by facet and
Face by Face to that one immaterial

diamond-sharp call that goes out
echo after echo across each

mountaintop of us that the sky rests on
and where eagles catch their

prey in their talons in
midair and continue flying

So catch us in our attempts to flee
in our weak fluttering and in Your

greater swoop fly with our hearts
in your tight grasp

swifter than light

3

In the dark I hear the
sizzle of the sea in my ears

Is that you Lord?

I see a streetlamp's slant of
light across the ceiling

Is that Your Merciful beam?

And the vast dimension of space in
sounds outside the window from it seems

all directions at once

the barks from across town
from one end to the other and

rooster crows and their triple-crow echoes

*Is that You Lord crossing this
world with Your distinct Presence*

proving beyond doubt Your love for us?

It all gets louder then fades away
but its echoes remain

*Are these Your traces Lord
still hanging in the air?*

*Reverberations of Your endless
renaissance everywhere?*

Never a dull moment —
and You always near?

4

Don't let me sleep Lord
but come with me into that

darkness

You've been with me from the first
and from before the first

and you'll be with me after the
last gasp

So though You'll never let me go
Lord let me know You won't do so

and in these aches of days each
counted like a tomb

across a graveyard filled with its
several animations suddenly stilled

let Your emanations always wake me
even now as I

bend again into sleep
to enter Your sky

                                                        11/5

HIS VOICE

I want each poem to supersede
every other poem I've written

in power in light in impossible perfection
to get closer to Allah

though only Allah can say if I'm
anywhere near

and if it's His Voice I hear

> 11/5

EVERYTHING IS AUTO-SUGGESTION

Everything is auto-suggestion
Except Allah

Everything is out one door
and in another

except Allah

Everything is looking out one window
And the world is gone

Except Allah

Geese fly overhead trees
burst into flame

the world turns to a crisp
again and again

the bird of paradise
blooms its neon

flowering into other worlds
than this one

Darkness surrounds us
and Allah

surrounds all darkness

Everything perishes
Every face knuckle-bone

delirium extravaganza

Everything
Down to the last and final

tent peg

In a downpour as quiet
as shifting sand

Everything
except Allah

HE COMES RUNNING
A Turkish Sojourn — A Book Inside a Book

INTRODUCTION

Turkey is a place I might not have visited, having entered Sufic Islam via the Habibiyya Tariqa of Shaykh Muhammad ibn al-Habib (*rahimahu'llah*) in 1970, and through various visits to the great awliya of Morocco and Algeria, finding my spiritual center aligned most resonantly with the ways, practices and illuminations of North Africa. But we were all reading Arberry's translation of *The Discourses of Rumi* in the 60s in Berkeley, and when I bought the Nicholson volumes of Rumi's *Mathnawi* at Shambala Bookstore on Telegraph Avenue, I knew I'd found the apex of possible spiritual poetry, a notion that has only deepened with time. So behind everything has always been a connection, not uncommon it's true, with Mevlana Rumi as poet, teacher and saint.

With an invitation at the beginning of May, 2002, to visit a modern exponent of the Turkish way, Faruk Dilaver, through poet/saint Yunus Emre, and Rumi's mode of thought and indirect instruction, I accompanied a group of wayfarers there. In their honor, I made an intention to record my visit with poems in strict *ghazal* form, resulting in *The Flame of Transformation Turns to Light, Ninety-Nine Ghazals Written in English*. A number of them record the lightning-bolt embrace and its aftermath I felt upon entering Rumi's tomb in Konya, having so anticipated the visit from Berkeley on.

A second visit, again to meet and sit with Faruk Abi, in September of 2003, resulted in the book of poems, *Love is a Letter Burning in a High Wind*, with its favorite opening poem, *On the Road to Konya*, and a number of poems written in and off Rumi's tomb itself, as well as in the nearby memorial tomb of Shams, and others written during our travels to such places as Capadoccia.

Then most recently, in November of 2013, my wife Malika and I were invited to accompany dear friends to Istanbul, where Faruk would be visiting many of his Yunus Emre circle in people's houses (with often lavish dinners and décor) and listen long into the night to his *sohbets*, or talks, attended by wall to wall beloveds hanging on his every word, filled with wonderful and passionate zeal. Not knowing any Turksh, and many of the "translators" knowing only a curious English, with some superb exceptions, I found myself inspired to write poems from the prevailing atmosphere of such open-ended and deep spirituality.

Early in our stay, and after a tour of Istanbul's magnificent mosques, we went to lunch, where I noticed a tray of cut papers (6X4 inches in fact) by a telephone, for taking notes, easily fit in the pocket — a little pile of which I availed myself. Then one evening of talks I took out a page and wrote the first of what would result in this chronological series of poems written over the period of our two-week stay, intentionally keeping to only one poem per page, in free form not as formal but perhaps as stringently limiting as the *ghazals* from my first visit. Something ignited, the forced brevity, the nights of hearing various decipherments of the Turkish, snatches and bits of the sweet and sometimes fierce wisdom from Faruk, the strong love in the air — as well as from some of the other trips we took, the Black Sea, the markets, etc. I ended up with the fifty short poems I now present, each here on their own page, line by line as they were written. Hopefully they focus heartfelt fragments of The Path to Allah, love of His Prophet Muhammad, *salallahu alayhi wa sallam*, and His living sages, those physically present and those absent, with us in God's creation until the end of time.

(*The additional poems,* Myths We Never Knew, *were written during the same sojourn directly onto my iPad, a kind of experiment unusual for me who always writes in notebooks in longhand, with pen.*)

February, 13, 2014

Allah says: "I am as My servant expects Me to be,
and I am with him when he remembers Me.
If he thinks of Me, I think of him.
If he mentions Me in company,
I mention him in even better company.
When he comes closer to Me by a handspan,
I come closer to him by an arm's length.
If he draws closer to Me by an arm's length,
I draw closer by a distance of two outstretched arms
nearer to him.
If my Servant comes to me walking,
I go to him running."

— Hadith Qudsi (*Al-Bukhari)*

"Multiply yourself by zero."

— Baji Tayyaba Khanum

1

The exercise of diminishment
increases to a zero in which
all the flowers of the sacred
send out aromatic pods and
leaves of the Ninety-Nine
Names of God

If the five elements intrude
fold each one inside the other
on the great angelic wheel
that slices into the
Magnetic Mountain
in the space of no space
and swallow its drops into a
heart free of both earth and
heaven

2

If you destroy a portion of the good
increase in zones of generosity

and the sharp dragon's tail will
shrivel to lizard length
and soon disappear under a leaf

Mannequins in God's fancy shops
could be said to be facing

eternity or simply turning their
rigid backs on the world

As they maintain absolute silence
we can only speculate on their

sincerity or wonder if they
in fact know more than we do

3

A little bowl of spinach
across from the leather shop
carries with it odors of a
greener world than this one
even as it comes from the
greenness of this one

Fresh spring water right off
the busy street carries within it
rainbows from the spray of
waterfalls crossing each other
in paradisiacal arcs

If you see a face looking
back at you your surprise
is nothing compared to its

as the spray water dissolves
the outlines of both

4

Overhead lights don't
exist in gypsy camps that aren't
stars in decipherable
constellations whose illumined
walls are traversed by centaurs
and roaring lions

Reflections on marble don't
exist in deserts whose baked
dunes change places with
mirages of cities lost in the
sophistications of their deaths
as their gates close for
the night

Real walls tumble down
as real trees grow tall
and sway in real wind

5

Has the cloud of love hovered
over the countries of death?
Are blasted house fronts and

crumbled doors signs of love
gone sour? Have the people
run wild through streets
in search of God's love or in
flight from it? Is its Light
too bright to bear? Are even
sips of it too much for some?

Will we all sizzle down to a
regular surf at last at love's
ocean's edge to endure its
delirious intensities? A dark
sky slashed from end to
end in light?

6

Lungs are cutting through forests
of cigarette smoke in close
quarters with windows
shut tight

No relief in sight

Breath in short intakes to
filter what smoke can be
filtered but certain vipers
seem to thrive on it and
grow longer and stronger
as we shrink and become

weaker

Will the windows to let in
fresh air never be opened?

7

A rolling road slowly rises
out of dark blue cloud

Various figures can be seen
moving slowly to and fro
inside the cloud as they find a
way to the road to begin a
long trek out
though their equipment be
frail and in deep need of repair
before they attempt it and the
road rise suddenly
at a steep angle upward

Carry the papers and the
stick given you and an
owl's scrutiny and a
cougar's stealth

8

A king is coming

Not the king of a country but
a king of himself and a
vastness inside his kingdom of self
for the One King to reside and
flow through to the empty
kingdoms outside himself where
the One King also resides whether
or not they know and lay
waste to the night-crawlers
who lay in wait to waylay those
waiting for the One King to
arrive

A king is coming

He will arrive soon and
everything will change

9

Sometimes the King comes and
sometimes the circus comes
and they both occupy the
same tent surrounded by
tame lions and clowns

Sunlight after a day of rain
can show us which is which

I saw a flock of crows

and a flock of geese

The crows were having a
powwow in the treetops

The geese were following their
leader in the sky south for
the winter glittering with
wintry light

10

The nearby dogs are silent
the distant dogs still bark

This is only some of the things you can
pick out in the dark

A bridge of flame is falling
the night sky fills a glass

the earth is trembling in
expectation of what will come to pass

The captain of the ship
has long gone down below

Only God can steer us to
safety now before we'll have to row

11

At the dawn call to prayer from
the nearby lovely spindly-minareted
mosque crossing *adhans* from other
minarets by loudspeakers all the
dogs near and far begin to yip and
howl and bark in chorus as well

Are they Satan's dogs howling in
disrespect to keep the believers
away or are they God's dogs
joyously celebrating the calls
and joining in annunciatory glee

extending the call to the dog
world and any other sleepy
canines within the ears' both
short and triangular or long and floppy
compass of sound?

12

There were chickens and geese
and strange pointy goose-tongues as
they hacked their greetings or
admonitions at us through the
fence

Then later sheep and straggly
odorless rose bushes and a
bright orange flower with
sheep in the distance

A bare and barren landscape
with dry grasses rough hedges and
bluish mountains in the distance
that Van Gogh with bamboo pens
and sepia and India ink could
bring to vibrant life with quick
stipple strokes and a thousand
heartfelt dots

13

While awaiting the king's arrival
seventy foals were born in
a barn filled with illuminated
straw

Three cities submitted to a very
short tyrant's army because of
the size of the brass buttons on
their uniforms

Hair and nails got longer and the
seasons changed

Little by little a fair outline of the

king emerged and some said
they saw it between the forest
trees and others that they ate
with it just after dawn

Maybe the king was already
with us all along

14

In a well-appointed room
with multiple conversations
the children's footsteps could be
heard above them on the wooden
floors

Swans floated on the word
streams and some ducks
also slept with their heads
tucked under their wings

Echoes intruded and had their
own opinions but few paid
them the attention they were
due

Voices rose and fell
Doors opened and closed

No one moved in the lexicons
of the air

15

When the horses came through
the landscapes they came through
flowed from their manes

In their eyes we saw the vision
of Allah they saw and wept

Large brown pools and every
phase of the moon in an
instant stretched from the
first to the last eternity
and back again in a moment
hanging from the eyelashes of
landscapes that had become
horses in leafy motion as
stationary as trees

Only Allah sees Allah
and only He knows Himself

Everything else is air and water

16

When he spoke in a language
only some of us knew there was
a screen of lights and shadows

and unseen flights of meaning
seeking their sources
in the hearts inside our ears
and ears inside our
hearts

But no one could repeat
word for word what he said

And waters of a golden
comprehension rose above
our knees that know
prostration and our foreheads
that practice submission

17

To die before you die is to find
a meaning that stays meaning
that when north becomes south
and west becomes east meaning
stays in its high crystal
receiving the light it emits

When we become beside ourselves
we become most and nothing at
one stroke

If we step out of one space in
our original shape the showers

of His Mercy descend and fill
the space of all emptiness until
nothing is left and everything is
just as it is in Allah's Grace

18

At the stroke of One
His Mercy began

At the stroke of two the
world was full

At the stroke of three
space gleamed

At the stroke of four
all looseness tightened

And at the stroke of five
a stream of bees visited the
lips of the Beloved to spread
His sweetness through the
creation and let its drops
drip into our hearts

Numbers dissolved into essences
and essences dissolved into
all of us at once again

19

How can He be otherwise
than where we are?

Hearing news of Him was the
end of knowledge of Him

We began unreeling this thread
and will end by reeling it in
again and the end is in the
beginning and its end and
beginning and span between
are from Him Who is only
where we are and whose
only "where" is where we are

It is a hollow thread and
shines

And is a Voice more than a
thread and a shattering of
Light in secret places

20

We have come here to be
where He is

Hello to distance
Be in our hearts!

Hello to the winds of where we
are

Take us to Him Who is where we
are

Tell Him we are here to be
where He is which is where
we are

If there was anywhere where
He wasn't there would be
nowhere where He is

But that is not possible
so He is Here

21

In the sweet aftermath
dogs bark and a rooster crows
his hens around him meekly
pecking the ground

And night drapes her long
gowns over the world and
fastens them with the moon's
crescent

Has the king's robe caught on a
chair leg as he passed by?
Has a fluff of his ermine fallen
from his robe onto our Path?

Is the air around our bodies and
in our lungs the same?

Mirrors have shifted and fallen
into their silver backings to
reveal the rose garden they
always were
in sunlit shafts

22

Since I couldn't understand what
he was saying I decided to
write down what he said

At this the geese who had
honked at us in the afternoon
took flight in distinct and
elegant formations until
the skies were white with
them

Not knowing his words I
listened for their echoes and
found the well they were

emitting from not far from
where I was and was
not

An authenticating seal floated down
like a goose feather and stamped its
circle of light here

23

When love drives a furrow
through death's pasture the
only crop that grows
is lovers

Don't tell me sunlight and rain
don't reach these fields or
that black crows with the
knives and forks of their beaks
will gobble up the seeds and
leave it fallow

Even fallow yields results as
one vibration in love's direction
is enough to effect the required
atoms for all good to grow

"He comes running"

Even from the farthest dry

outpost or the seeming-most
bare and piebald station
death-mound vacancy

24

Oh son of the beloved
stand in the center of this walking
though I only caught a few
rare glimpses of your face
always hooded in God-Snow
and God-Light at the far end
where you started down the hill

You left your inviolable impression
in the air no one dares enter
but from which all may draw
any treasure they can whether of
glass or silence or the dance of
shadows against a wall

Even in broad daylight and the
sun directly overhead your
light is greater by God

No one can forget the sound of
horses cantering away

25

The king sits under any tree and
on any rock in any windblown
landscape on earth or heaven
to converse with crickets and
bluebirds in their daily passages

No subjects escape his notice
though he may not mention them
by name but only elude to
their velvet edges as they age
and wither

He's always news fresh and
alive and up to the moment

His notice is Allah's notice
and each special ant under
his gaze carries the sunlight
of longevity and the moonlight
of death's sugary banquets

26

Heartfelt advice begins in one
and leaps across to another who's
asked in all heartfelt openness

In the air it takes the color of
possible storms and desert
stillnesses in which no fox ear
twitches nor scorpion digs

Will its balm reach the
recipient's bones and enter their
marrow enough to transform
today's tomorrow?

Will buildings in the mind block
the sun or cast longer shadows?

Alleyways behind the elegant
facades of the heart wriggle and
zigzag into out-gates and into
more breathable atmospheres

27

The heart came out of the body
and spoke and by heart we mean
that living forest of swinging birds
and musical knowledges interwoven
among the leaves of ancient trees

By the heart we mean the heart
of the heart which is a boundless
ocean waiting for the touch of God
to illumine under the brightest sky

By heart what is meant is what
already knows the truth the
way trees know to grow

When the singer began to sing a
voice from far away came up
through his throat where many
drunk dervishes have vanished
and reappeared

28

A brave and ruined man
became a sudden flying bird
whose wingspread spanned the
skies

He closed his eyes in a crowded
room and a chorus of voices
trembled through his fluttering
voice that drew water from
invisible wells and spun
honey from invisible hives

Salaams from a shore
beyond water and an ocean
beyond waves

A sky leans down and takes
us by our hands to draw us
up

29

Sometimes the dawn comes
up so silently you don't notice
that its tissues of gold have
slid over everything with the
just-as-it-is-ness of everything
placid in its light

It's been said a dragon sleeps
in the mountain unkilled and
undefeated although no one's
seen it firsthand except
those who've set out to rid
us of its menace

Some people also disappear
into daylight and are never
seen again

A weak post-dawn crowing of
a rooster can just be heard

30

The peace you see in his
eyes is that he's always happy

The peace you see in his eyes is that
he's always satisfied

The peace you see in his eyes is that he's
always with Allah

If a giant camel came or a small
yellow taxi he'd get on or in it
all the same to go where he
wants and where he wants is Allah

He knows Allah is First and Last
First before firstness and Last
beyond lastness and He is the Outwardly
Manifest and the Inwardly Hidden

The peace in his eyes is the tangerine
he's eating and the tea he's sipping

31

The least fly lands on a
shiny black Mercedes trunk lid
and feels at home

Sunlight expands to all far
corners at once with God's
Name on its chapped lips

Waters keep rushing to
forward places over rocks

Mankind takes a breath
and lets it out again

I think mountains will rip
themselves open out of love for
Allah and plains will
become plainer to shrink
themselves before His Majesty

32

At one point the King drops
everything and emerges from his
separate body as pure spirit

No birds fall out of their trees
but the skies coalesce above him
and hover to watch over his
sudden nakedness

Orchestras in far islands awaken
and sit behind their miraculously
tuned instruments and at a tiny
twig crack begin their heavenly
music

The King keeps going and coming
into and out of himself and
every other self in creation
since he's left his own self
behind

33

Pine nuts come from
little scrubby pine trees with long
dark green needles along the side of the
road

We all come from Allah

Coffee scent from a steaming cup
of coffee can be traced back to
its source set out for us to drink

We can follow traces from our
own obstreperous beings to our
Magnificent and Beauteous Lord

Here's something — sunlight
glittering in an afternoon ride to the
Black Sea diffuses in the air and
igniting our vision everywhere also
can be traced back to the Living
God Life-Giver over all

34

What beasts raise their heads?

What lions in thickets peer through
to watch for movements in the

sun? What gazelles of pure love
whose black pool eyes contain
dark truths of God's Wondrousness
stand too still and vulnerable to
be missed by such patient
leonine scrutiny?

God pounce on me!
Carry me to your lair!

How many earthly breezes and
watery dawns shall I continue
to stand in before I'm taken?

The green oasis shimmers and
the desert stretches around it
to the end of time

35

The King is camped not far
from here in the middle of the
road so that everyone must
acknowledge his existence

For those who have said
the King is not alive they have to
go around a camp of huge pointed
tents of all the hues in the world
and the King's great singers
harmonizing from tent to tent

For those who do know he's with us
there are people in each tent to make
them feel at home with special
banquets and the King visits each
tent personally each night by
special lamplight and gazes into
their eyes with loving gazes

Some go through the camp this
way and others go around but the
King is a patient King
and loves them both

36

If you enter the King's room
there's nothing there
There's only something there when
the King's there

If you take the King away the
nothingness of things without the
King appears

Everything depends on the King

Things may think they can do without
the King and that He appears and
disappears but that's only in the
realm of "things"

He's made it to seem that way
It lets things seem to go their
own way

But their own way that they
don't own is the way with the
King who owns all ways

Everything happens with the King

37

The King couldn't come Himself
or leave His place of origin so He sent
a few messengers of the first rank who
changed the world and many messengers
of the second rank who keep the
machinery running

Everyone knows of the messengers of the
first rank and their names have
interior light in daylight or at
night that illumines the jungle paths

Messengers of the second rank may be
less well-known since many take
menial jobs and may be seen in
unusual places that may even seem
unkingly but their eyes and words
tell the story and their visits

alleviate pain and elevate
hearts

38

There's a black door

Who stands inside the black door?

Who resides within the black door?

Is there a star in the black door?

Do stars come out inside the black door?

Are all the planets inside the black door?

It stands here in the blackest of blackness

It stands open in the blackest of blackness

It is one door

There is nothing outside it

Outside it there is no blackness

Inside it is a single light

which is everything

39

The lips of the messengers of the
first rank are moving still

The lips of the messengers of the
second rank keep being born

The faces of the messengers of the
first rank rise and enter the
phases of the moon

The faces of the messengers of the
second rank may look out at us
from unexpected places as
common as daylight or as
unique as ecstasy under a
wide and gold-flecked banyan
tree or behind the window of
a shop

But the eyes of the messengers of both
first and second rank are the
same

And their hearts contain only Allah

40

The prophets enter the world from
Allah's Presence
through the black door

The saints enter Allah's Presence
through the black door
from the world

No edges exist from both
directions and the frame
of the black door is more black doors
of which there is only One

I see a black car under a
maple tree under a blue sky

The moon's almost invisible in
the blue sky

Each leaf stands out in the
clear air

Voices in the car are music
to the ears

41

The journey takes place and

before you know it you're
on it

What landscapes are flying out of
your eyes? What marketplaces
filled with hand-turned beads
and glass balls on strings! What
rainbow-colored things in stalls
like docile beasts waiting for
purchase!

And what sacred wells and ancient
trees planted in saintly places!

What darkness and light!

And then before you know it
the journey's end is in sight! Trumpets
in the distance! A lovely softness
to the edges of everything! All
signs pointing upward!

42

So when I die will I get
out of here like a slippery eel
or like a cranky antique
dealer who locks his doors for
fear someone might steal his
candelabras? This and that

thought pile up about this and that
and how it gets distributed or
destroyed

Words words words in books and
manuscripts derelict or headed
to good homes where there's a
warm reception and understanding

Do we leave rubble behind or
perhaps one polished brass
sphere that reflects the world
in its pure insubstantiality?

43

There are people all over the
world who stop periodically
every day to face God to thank
and praise and loosen the world's
hold on them and increase the
unseen splendor's attraction
for and to them all hopefully and
hopelessly for God's sake like
the waves of the sea do

and small creatures cleaning their
feelers and lions on hilltops
roaring and babies looking up at
their mothers full of trust and
love beyond their comprehension do

We pray like waves of the sea do

and God sees each wave as it
breaks and disappears

as we do

44

One day a Prince was
served a single tomato
when he was expecting a feast

His first reaction that poured
up through him was rage
until he saw that his rage
was the color of the tomato
only less bright and less
shiny

He looked again and while the
astonished courtiers held their
breath the Prince saw the tomato
transform into an angel of
brighter colors and greater shininess

who opened its wings that
extended from pole to pole
and polished the world

45

I've been in a house that
turned itself inside-out for
love of Allah and His Prophet
peace be upon him until there
was no room for anything but
love

The walls poured tears and the
floors prostrated the foreheads
of their boards in deeper submission

The tables groaned until a
feast was spread for the poor
and sheep were herded past its
chairs into courtyards of grace

So many angelic suspensions
rose that the roof
had to hold its breath until
the sky soothed its shingles
and peace descended

46

Even just a whispered breath
from the heart is enough as a
burnt offering in the ancient sense
and a pure offering in the
present tense

We look out from under eyes
that are lowered and bow
foreheads that are always in
prostration and our limbs from
head to toe shiver with God's
excitement

Then even the ocean senses these
seismic shifts and curls back
fringes of surf in acknowledgment

Even the fishes in the bottomless
dark passing each other with
neon headlamps know these
heartfelt whisperings for Allah

47

Ten minutes to the next
prayer and an earthquake
could blast the floor and walls

Nine minutes to the next prayer
and veils of light and darkness
could show Allah to Himself
through the eyes of our hearts

Eight minutes to the next prayer
and thoughts of our parents could
ease them in their graves

Seven minutes to the next prayer
and elephant infants could be born

Six minutes to the next prayer and
water could recede into the ground
everywhere

Five minutes to the next prayer and
suddenly Lover and Beloved are
One only and no second face is
ever possible anymore

48

Four minutes to the next prayer
and life bursts out in inane
conversations stray thoughts and
howling dogs asking God's
mercy for humankind

Three minutes to the next prayer and
a sudden convoy of angelic
trucks brings fresh water to
refugees in crowded camps

Two minutes to the next prayer
and forests become renewed with
great trees and bromiliads in bloom

One minute to the next prayer

and Azrael could appear facing
us directly and showing us the way
to Allah

The next prayer has come and we
stand in a row

as present as possible

49

Then the King can be seen as
a country groom among his
horses and sunlight coming in
through chinks in the barn

Don't be deceived

Push aside his leathern vest
and vestments of a rare
cloth studded with true star-
particles are revealed

When he rides off the sorrow of
his departure on the part of
the townspeople is palpable
and he leaves behind the living
chain of his sayings his
observations and his silences

No one can forget the sound
of hooves cantering away

50

Do the arrival and departure
of God's Friend have the same
impact?

Joy and expectation and grief
all at once? Nothing
remains as it was in their
precincts

What they know precedes
creation and remains long
after it dissolves

It's joy and expectation and grief
for ourselves both their
infinite loss and explosion unto Allah's
Magnificent Beauty rolling into
gorgeous sky and green
hills where before was only

a sameness under hidden
starlight

MYTHS WE NEVER KNEW

1

The stars used to be speckles on a dolphin's back
leaping through oceanic snow in sunlight

unseen by any but God

reflected in the mirrors of His ever-rolling waves
turned upside-down by time

2

Ever-rolling waves never look back

and never repeat themselves once they've
left the coil of their uncurling momentum

sliding across the aquatic dorsals of just
barely submerged leviathans

3

If we wonder where these arabesque thoughts come from
these caged beasts rattling the bars of their cages in
curious cadences

these front porches of words whose houses behind them
extend back to infinity

these emergences from silence whose famous cave
sometimes emits wisdom but most often among men
emits puffs of multi-colored smoke

And if we more attentively wonder where real
words of ever-rolling wisdom come from that astonish
any sensitive ears with the sterling of their silver
and the carats of their gold

we need only look with our hearts at how sunlight works
as it slides through every blade of grass to
warm the earth

or how soon babies learn to speak their fears and amazements
with mother-love tutoring and a few wrong moves corrected

Is it all the same swirl as ocean waves
whose energies come

from their own depths?

Whose eyes are always upon us
if not God's?

Whose ears hear everything?

Whose voice is the voice of the entire world?

Whose actions are all actions at once in every world and
all worlds at all times
everywhere?

A tiny glimpse may bring it all to bear

A soft whisper is enough to move mountains
and shake the air

4

Whales rose up to command the orbits
of great and small
significant and inconsequential

so that all things may have their
ends in their beginnings

their starts in their stops
pauses in continuations
sweetness in sour

God holding us to these things to see our faces
glow or glower

as all orbits make their serpent rounds
from car wheels to Saturn's rings turning —

whales below in God's deeps below that
churning

5

That air around the earth is a spherical envelope
of angelic breathing

And when an airplane descends from flight slowly
down through clouds
it's all angel exhalations melodiously popping
in our ears

to get our rhythmic bearings

6

To get on with the threshing and plowing
The shaping and dissolving

The way waves crest and slide away
And clouds gather and sigh into nothingness

All it takes is a high heart
And eyes for beauty

And a silent mouth
And limbs that do God's work

In the back currents and forward flows
Into eternity and emptiness

Whose light dazzles and silence deafens
With its sweet amorous delicacies

7

We always wonder about death when it's
death that wonders about us

and why we are so oblivious to its charms
its whinnying stallions ready to take us to the

farthest horizon in its blaze of glory
or the firefly into the interior of its

flickering light

as night settles down over the land
letting its soft cloth down slowly so slowly

we barely notice the windows have gone
black and the rooms turned to silence

lips hands feet and shadows
dissolved into silent lips

but the eyes awake
on the other side

filled with delight

8

The doorway for all of us
is the same as for all of us

The little airplane of gold and dark chromium
dips its wings and we climb aboard

and out it goes through the
doorway for all of us

but the stairway to the doorway
is different for all of us

and the stairway on the
other side of the doorway

that leads down from that doorway

is how we are both before and
after that doorway

somewhere in the throat
somewhere in the heart

is different for all of us

how we do and how we are before we
get to the doorway

and who we are at the very moment when we
stand in that doorway before

going through

afloat or on our knees
and if we've been really on our knees

before we get to that
doorway

9

In simplicity is God's clarity
as if looking across a great prairie

directly into endless blue sky
in the heart and in the eye

of the eternal beholder
Who is Himself the Holder

of each tentacle and feeler
each sweet thought that steels

across the empty screen
that lies before after and between

each thing

TIME HOLDS ITS BREATH

ETERNITY

> Eternity is in love with the productions of time
> — William Blake, *The Marriage of Heaven and Hell*

1

Sad alabasters and perky
peacock feathers turn to

rust in our hands

Wave our hands across their smeared
faces and see angelic glances through

silver eyes

No one will see you when you
disappear from sight

yet you persist in existence
greater than before

rung around with neon rings and
sounds of glass like trembling water

Don't rush things ancient ones
let one foot fall behind

the other on the mountain passes
and fresh sunlight warm you

as dust filters through our fingers
each flake calling out our name as it

drifts backwards in the air

unreconstituteable

and a sweet nothingness

God willing when it happens
we'll still be there

2

Bright splinter! Do you
always seek behind appearances?

Are you dark metal under the smoke?
Sharp glare behind a smile?

We scan you to be our torchlight here
every spider corner revealed

every turn disclosed

Why have I only seen you now?
Is this the meltdown of the snow?

Is this the Great Dissolve?

3

Eternity shimmers in the room among the
bright solid furniture that is the

furniture of Eternity the bookcases and lamps
the bed I wake from and the

sound of the silence here that is its
child the swirling ocean of time

washing us in its blessings in constant
motion of cylinder within cylinder of

intangible turning invisible to the touch
in which we age minute by minute

inwardly forward but motionless in
Eternity impossible to calculate except in

angelic terms whose bright silver
dazzles the mind beyond its usual

earthly limitations whose walls and
doors and streets and skies are

sweetly blasted apart by the dimensions of
Eternity and we

live in it unbeknownst to us else we'd
faint at the pure nothingness we are

and God's Magnificence always facing us
beyond even Eternity's confines and paltry

measurements to show us anything but His
resplendent Face in absolutely

everything that is in its instant of being
the Living One from end to end and all

height and depth possible to what
has no existence except in Him

Alone Light upon Light right in
front of us and deep within us

eternally shimmering
as time holds its breath

11/15

CAP AND BELLS

Cap and bells won't keep the party going
but throwing your lot with the lotless

and your state with the stateless

Keeping the zero that we are rising and
expanding around us

until sailboats in silhouette on
sunset's mauve horizon are also

engulfed in its strangeness and
death's beauteous ermines of light

night's ink-black darkness our Nirvana
whose profile faces always away

to uttermost spacelessness
speechless in pure gracefulness

God's snowy lace across our last original
faceless primordial

placelessness

11/16

TIME HOLDS ITS BREATH

Time holds its breath when a
saint walks underneath its gaze

and space makes room in both
earthly and heavenly dimensions

and all that is alive leans close
to listen to a saint's breath

its pauses and continuations
and words that may float out on it

or silences that may be held in God's
honor in great circles only deer

may safely cross with their wide
black eyes and quivering nostrils

and dainty hooves capable of sudden
power to attack or leap away

"All this takes place in our hearts"
say the saints in chronological unison

wherever they roam with eagles of light
flying above their heads with fresh

high news held in golden talons
and far mountain ranges imaged in

eagle eyes able to scan from horizon to
horizon in a single sweep sunset to

dawn and dawn to sunset
wherever saints sleeplessly wander

and through whatever doors into rooms
they may happen to enter

always among and always
beyond us

whenever and wherever
they may happen to enter

11/17

THE UNIVERSOUL CIRCUS

1

In the UniverSoul Circus we
saw yesterday afternoon under a

great pitched bright red and yellow
big top that looked like a

Turkish fantasy illustration
with scalloped panels and pointed tip

a magician put a bodacious spangly
woman in a large glass box pulled a

red cloth over it and hoisted it into the
air in the middle of the single

center ring

and at a grand and loudly fanfare'd
swish of his wand the red cloth was

flung open and a huge live tiger stood in the
box filling the space with no sign at

all of the woman in there with it
and the magician took his jubilant

bow to the audience and the box with
prowling tiger was lowered and

rolled out the performer's exit to the
screams and applause of the audience

and whisked away

2

What are we to do with this illusion?
Lady into tiger tiger into

Eiffel Tower Eiffel Tower into scattered
bats against a night sky

And so it goes continually
The Metropolis of Metamorphosis in which

we dwell half shrunk and half expanding
the soul of us like an old fashioned

dirigible floating slowly across the earth
casting even an eerie shadow on the

continents as they bask in the sun letting their
rivers flow into their various seas

But the trick's done with a false wall up at
first behind which the tiger is enclosed

and once the curtain is up around it
the woman slips down through a narrow trap

door on the floor
and pulls the wall down at the same time

releasing the tiger into the main
area of the box so they actually

never meet lady and tiger and we can only
hope it all works without a hitch!

Tiger paws thumping above the
scrunched woman under the floor!

Circuses are predicated on it being perhaps
the last performance for

all of them the last
tightrope walk the last

tumbler flung into the air in loops to the
shoulders of a man standing on the

shoulders of a man who's standing on the
shoulders of a man standing in the ring

But each act's perfected defiance is
if it's the last moment alive or the next one

as each moment's precision by God's Grace

falls minutely and
perfectly into place

11/19-20

THE ROWERS ALL ROW

The rowers all row in synchronization
moving forward and back in

perfect time

Each day follows another as only it can
all things falling into place

wandering up its stairs and down its
long streets

through doors into rooms and
out again

Never noticing the beast sleeping on its side
making huge smoke puffs with

each inhalation each flicker of eyelids

never noting the sparrows daintily
falling from the trees or the undainty

trees themselves noisily
falling in their forests

unheard

never noticing the tilt of the earth on its
axis having been flung into orbit and

lopsidedly spinning here this long and so
much longer

as the rowers pull and pull on their
extended oars in black waters

and black sky surrounds us
as only it can

nowhere else quite as snugly
nor as star-studded with glimmering

and our noses catching the scent of both
distance and nearness though maybe

no one's ever sneezed at a blip in Saturn's
rounding its established bend

each call of God to His incandescent Presence
heard across a fence of space and in a

glass lantern of time whose
light never goes out even as it

incessantly flickers

casting that eerie glow on our faces
as we age and

die away

11/22

DON'T TURN AWAY JUST YET

Don't turn away just yet
with so much more to go

the city adazzle with the
fires of sunset on its billion windows

oceans unrolling treasures from their
depths at our feet like

sly carpet salesmen each pattern
astonishing in its arabesque

complexities then vanishing away

You've never been here before in
quite this space or time

and you'll never be here again
so before the sides of this particular

box you're in disappear take a
deep breath and

savor their disappearance

meadows extending to the far
edge and beyond

the way the sky tacks down at the
farthest point and is more like

extended earth with all within it
simultaneously singing

11/24
(this poem retrieved intact from dream)

OUR HEARTS ARE GONGS

To the surly landlord of the earth we say
don't worry you'll get your due one day

To the sky's dazzle and transformations
we also rise through transitional stations

To the air around us and deep inside us
can your sweet nothingness abide us?

To the restless rotations in various oceans
our hearts are also in constant motion

To the darkness surrounding our bustling planet
flesh light as air soul strong as granite

To the sound of the flute that calls us home
God's origin and goal and why we've come

To silence at the start and silence that follows
our flight as swift as the flight of swallows

To remaining long after the earth is gone
in eternity's orchestra our hearts are gongs

11/25

EVERYTHING THAT CAN BE SAID

Everything that can be said
behind a face of silence in a

thick dark wood whose trees
whisper

Everything on the tips of our
tongues or in the hidden flaps

of our hearts unsaid and unsayable
as silent as a plain of giraffes

silently galloping under migrating
geese

All we hear in our own echoing wells
resounding up its walls to our own

heart's ears

none of which we can really say at all
only God can say

in the shadows everything casts on a
wall of light

that never ends

and we also
unendingly saying and unendingly

silent
our eyes in their orbits of

silently seeing
and our hearts that

surround us in their
reverberant being

 11/26

THE SERPENT THAT SIZZLES

The serpent that sizzles under our skin
like an inner tattoo

attended by malevolent elves

who makes us afraid when we
enter a dark wood and

shrivels up to worm size to
turn us away from light

and who's given many names by
every theology

and who lounges in the sun inside us
to show us how friendly it

really is after all
thawing out again to its

full length and looking out through our
beady green eyes with its

sour beams
to appall each thing we see

as we see each thing

is charmed by the flute of our love
to go back to its basket

and leave us alone
our love so great for Allah alone

all living gets swept up in it
putting out those serpentine eyebeams and

dark exhalations
shedding its dead skin as if

burnt away in our greater amorous conflagration
back in the ground under wet leaves

in the landscape of our selves that
knows every terrain

guarded over by a sunlight so fine
like angel's hair woven to

invisibility seeping its serpent netting
past our bone palace

to our very marrow
Light upon Light in

total command over all

and even black night blacker than
night a light up ahead

to guide us right to a perfect
pinpoint whose within us is now

before us so no serpent can
hiss in us even if it's

inside us

11/30

EATING STARS

Have you ever eaten a star?

Why should they be so far away we can
never know them?

I see their light radiate out of
mouths as well as eyes

Some open mouths and starlight flows
whereas as Blake says

some people speak and put
starlight out

Any distance between us and cosmos is
illusory

unless such proximity makes us uneasy
whereas extension is really our original

dimension for the whole human-birth-to
death-span panoply

Put our arms out between one
galaxy and the next

They float in blackness like suspended fireflies
in rainbow nimbuses more glowing because

the black they float in is echoing with
God's deep velvety endlessness

and we're these conscious flesh and
bone planets whose arms and

legs jut out and seem to place us in
space

Orbiting hearts don't know such
limitations in the

spaceless vastness of God's love manifest in
in and out breaths each

living thing from stone to star has
creating even the illusion of

time itself

whose only beat

is the heartbeat

12/1

IF WE PUT A THOUSAND BRIDGES

If we put a thousand bridges in place
could we cross into the Next World

in our present living bodies? Would they be
of the finest spun glass

shimmering already with its
otherworldly shimmers? Another

moonlight and sunlight shining off their
cables and their beams?

There are those who cross easily already
and come back with news

and if we want to taste its atmospheres
it may be that we can in our

present mortal state
somehow almost visible in the

felt soft thuds of our heartbeats inside our
mortal body's cavity

and the domed skin of consciousness
at the moment of waking

when nothing seems that far
out of reach

But to be there
and look back from it!

Seeing these rough earthly landscapes
from its perspective

not space travel or
anything like it

nor even inner-space travel
but something else

and of God's conscious domain
with its buttery trees and gliding

rainbow rivers peopled with singing
and deep dimensions that shoot out in

all directions at once
and unimpeded view and unimpeded

travel domain after domain in
extra-spatial deliciousness

on bird's tongue and beast-eye
brightness

beyond our usual senses
and all our usual conceptions

a silveriness to things
and tremors as of deep throat-singing

and edge-lights as of distant
starlight to

everything
and a loving embrace at last

that takes away every
anxiety

knowing our true home
in that place and this

having been invited here
by God

in the first place

to this

12/3

THERE'S NOTHING TO BE DONE

There's nothing to be done but to
be where we are

No mirroring glass can be broken
that enters us

into a world brighter than this one

No sound can exceed high shrillness
to shatter a sky full of stars to

get us into God's Presence more than
where we are which is

in His time and space in which He
does not dwell but into which we've been

born and out of whose lifelong
embryo we'll be born again into

the next world that is also His in which
He does not dwell

But whose breezes laden with the most
exquisite perfumes can be sensed

when our souls will be sensate and our
senses will be of soul-light alone

in the radiant rays
at this moment alone that contains

all possible moments at once in its
divine compendium

                                                            12/13

WELL OF BLUE WATER

At the absolute bottom
of a well of blue water

shines a mirror of topaz
with a moon in its center

There's a sound of grinding
in the air above it

and a voice that mimics it
but whose words are distinct

and an ear that listens
by lowering it down

on a chain of starlight
that sings in two keys

The closer the ear gets
to the voice at the bottom

the stronger the heart beats
like a stallion of silver

When the landscape lightens
in the light of broad daylight

we stand at the well
with words written within us

and birds make an archway
that opens in heaven

where light rays originate
that shine on the earth

In the well now the sun shines
that spreads out everywhere

that we walk in and die in
singing its song

The eye closes above it
both sunlight and moonlight

inside out to everything
except to its depth

that goes on and on
into the next world

where we'll meet it again
singing God's song

12/14

YOUR WHOLE FACE

for Malika

There's a lapping all right at the
edges of the shore

coming from the next world
to this

a scattering of lights like the
afterimage of fireworks

in very black night
that also hails from there

And whispers behind words we hear
sonic double-image with dimensional

import

a stuttering forward of motions that
brings echoes from the next world

into this one like shadows against
dazzling marble or

lines of trees reflected upside-down
on a glimmering black lake

God's intertwined it into this one
seamlessly

sudden events and
sudden disappearances

how the sky seems to want to
burst its deepest secrets

especially in blazing sunsets
when the world

catches fire

or when you turn your whole face
to me and I can't

conceive of us
ever being

parted

12/20

SITTING ON TOP OF THE PLANET

I'm sitting on the top of the planet
thinking

*"What else is there to do
but sit here waiting for God?"*

Cites are all asleep under their fog
Restless hearts stand at their

windows smoking

Oceans lick sky with their
endless waves

My footprints have abandoned me
and people are silent or audibly

indecisive

The legs of the chair I sit on
bore down through the ground

I'll be on the other side of the planet
before long

and it will be all the same
same comings and goings

Same birth and death
celebrations

I wait for God Who's been
calling me all along

and I've felt myself
enwrapped in that call

moon face sun face
the same

from His perspective

Love and hate from that perspective
the same

trumped by God's love above all

ice horses melting by the
side of the road

Night falls to its knees
with the rest of us

in deep anticipation

12/21

SPHERE OF LIGHT

Waiting fifteen minutes to Fajr Prayer
just this side of the

end of the world
kaleidoscoping inward toward us all

escalators and fiery stairways
plummeting through purple smoke totally

overpopulated each step with
people fleeing what's all around and

inside us
except for occasional beings floating in

huge translucent spheres of a golden
light whose eyelids flutter slightly

at each explosion but whose
heartbeats are even louder than each

explosion and somehow
soothing in the smoke-blacked air

to everyone on their way upward
step by step out of the crumbly chaos

Buildings and mountains become
dancers in perfect choreography

in this perfectly silent room
at the starting point of Fajr

in Allah's perfectly executed fluttering
choreography each instant

in this sphere of light
in which all of us float

12/24

JOY IN GOD'S WORLD

Joy in God's world seems like at
such a premium and such a

rare commodity I mean really
wholehearted untrammeled joy at

the way light golden light outlines the
edge of each leaf and grass blade and

snort of horse or sneeze of
mouse behind wall or scampering across

ceiling heard from beneath
and a mountain breaking open in the

blue distance to expel its magma and
the ocean rearing up on its hind legs to

watch it as we
hold hands for fear and trembling the old

fear and trembling game at the outer
circles of mortality that seems to

dissolve circle by circle as we grow both much
less and so much more immortal after all

as we get nearer the center

and no dinosaur at the great gate to
greet us and no

pterodactyls wheeling in the sky above us as we
zoom backwards in uncountable

eons to our origins through various
galactic weathers and weak or strong

sunlights shielding our eyes with our
hands flat at our foreheads in that

poignant human way we have of
doing that

that no other animal does quite as
well (well maybe orangutans do it almost as

well)

and in all this the pure joy of it
unaccountable and irrational

as waves of God's love for it all
lap up through us and dissolve our own

circling separate beings
in His sea

IF WE COULD STEP INSIDE

If we could step inside the
perfect icy rooms of snowflakes

and meet the people thereof

in crazy rainbow jackets and
hats of fish tails

and walk along their dazzling geometric
corridors for a moment for this

very moment that seems so real and
to go on forever

before melting on someone's woolen sleeve
or on a bush or tree branch sticking up

skeletal black in a white sky

and hear its birds with their flute-like
iciness arching across from one linked

crystal tetrahedron to another each branch inside
the same as a branch in a

tree outside past which this
instantaneous snowflake falls

and peacefulness were to fall as
silently onto the world

and cover it

and we were to be that
snowflake of peace falling

onto the world
and covering it

1/4

THE CURSE OF A MOMENT

The curse of a moment can
echo down a thousand years

The blessing of a moment can
loop through the entire world

bringing together poor Nanking
noodle-maker with

young Romanian tightrope walker

or rabbit suddenly standing up
sniffing the air

or dust falling back to earth
after bison hoofs have passed

But a curse on the head of even the most
venal can cut through like a

rusted can lid and scar tender leaves of
hearts unknown and unremembered

taking lifetimes to heal

while a blessing sounded or unsounded
might shinny up the face of one or

two solitary souls on a solitary
back street in Italy or Cameroon under a

pitiless sun broken and alone
for one to turn to the other out of its

misery and notice a new sparkle in the
other's eyes for a moment and

feel suddenly safe

1/5

WINGS OF OBLIVION

How does pure light come down
over a brown day?

How does red flame eat through a
white page?

How do round things roll to a stop
and square things fall only once?

When we stand up how does the sky
make room for us?

If where the stars are they can see us
how brightly do we shine?

How do we all stay suspended
in this endless black night?

Do the end and beginning of it
matter to us?

How does the Lord Who is Aware of us
and knows us in great detail

greater detail than we can
know ourselves

and loves the gnat and firefly

dinosaur and rhinoceros

mountain streams with their
gush of running water

and the ways things end and the way
things begin

breath by breath and step by step
across the widest expanse

from tooth of smallest creature
to farthest star's extinguishment

over a red archway or black crevasse
whose time has come to be

extinguished
and sucked into a black hole

that doesn't seem to end
except turned inside-out inside us

over whom the Lord presides
Compassionate —

How does He
act without acting and

do without
doing? Though

He does it all?

How does this not make us
wild with love and dazzled by

bewilderment!

On tongues of angels and
wrapped in an indivisible wind?

Wings over oblivion!

1/6

SITTING WITH A SAINT

Sitting with a saint is
sitting on a cliff crumbling under you

and the sound of falling rocks and debris
is music to your heart's ears

though your self may not
hear it that way

and a crackling fire climbing up your
walls is a salamander cavalcade

the fire prophet Abraham saw turn into
singing read streamers in an updraft

and his sweat tiny bells making
melodic affirmations

Sitting with a saint is all the years backed up
before sitting with a saint

suddenly unrolling their
dusty prayer carpet before you

and every direction's God's unseen domain
invisible calligraphy all around you

and when you come away from

such an association as sitting with a

saint everywhere we look is
dusted with pollen and everything we

touch thereafter springs buds

1/7

NEW BOOTS

Angels don't need new boots
but if they had feet for them

they might wear the Mississippi lacing them
with flying catfish or small towns with just one

post office

They're open-ended at both ends
these terrestrial-celestial toe-twinklers

They fly on their own like goose migrations
They are fashion statements for the invisible

They weigh nothing when worn by angels though
no fulcrum anywhere could lift the earth from its orbit

Their laces link the stars in galactic loops
They enter God's halls on whispery slipperiness

that none but the Divine can distinguish from the
swish of ant feelers in the air

There are no new boots in all earth and heaven

Adam and Eve wore all the boots anyone anywhere would
wear forever when they wrapped their feet in leaves

leaving the garden for earthier climes

but angels above all wrapping themselves in clouds of light
have said or sung just about

all that can or be said or sung about new boots by just not
needing to wear them

except when lightning strikes
and you can see them in new shining

silvery skates streaking along instantaneous
flashing white lanes of electricity

1/8

DEEP FOREVERLAND

A life should have its circuitry
plugged in at both ends

its electricity not circular but
stretched in its infinite direction

crosswise across the cosmos
from life-source to death-source

taking in its arc account of
all that is

breath upon divine breath extended
from tree leaf green with life

to leaf of Paradise greener than even
life itself

bathed by a sun more central even
than our fiery orb

How does God see us
is how we should be

more who we are than
who we are to ourselves

in God's elegant tides
whose moonlit crests

reflect His Face
in the middle of nowhere

which is our true home
our own face gone in His Light

for all to see
alone in His populated world

one zebra at a time
out of obscurity's zigzags back into

obscurity again's hilarious solemnity
at peace in the bed we lie in

plugged in at both end's extensions
beyond them

and so blessed forever in His deep
Foreverland

1/11

I AWAKEN EACH DAY

I awaken each day to my
dubious achievements

and feel honored when the cat
sleeps on my sweater

forgotten on a chair

                                        1/12

HE WAITS BY THE GATE

He waits by the gate

or carves out the insides of an
elephant and

peers through the eyeholes

watches through flame-leaves that as they
leap up fully formed in new birth

destroy by burning

He looks at what's flat and sees depths
scans depths and sees fissures

descends through fissures and sees
light

knocks on the gate and unicorns exit
on which he rides and rides until they become

horses with no horn and usable bridles

able to move at ease among the
wandering populace who

fan out across the earth with their
distinctive foods cooked

just the way they like them
each population inviting him in

to taste their song

1/14

WITH THE SENSIBILITY OF GYROSCOPES

With the sensibility of gyroscopes
and the leathern wings of pterodactyls

making no shadows but that of the Matterhorn
when the sun first peaks and takes its

view of stasis the way an aged photographer
under his black cloth might suddenly stand

stock still and the world itself instead seem
in hectic motion

so consciousness itself when first
blinking awake might take account of itself

and prefer to skirt the margins of a dewy
paradise of greens and sulfur yellows

than say the back of bankrupt cities
whose people gaze blankly out dusty

screen doors having given up all hope
for any life at all much less a

better one

and swoop with a deft tilt the way a
plane does full of snoozing passengers

oceanward in a sky of the heart wider even than
the sky all around our earthen galaxy

that seems to go on forever with all it
contains of whispering orbits and exploding

eruptions in such sped-up slow motion it takes
millennia for the news to get to us

so in the same way as in this cluttered catalog
news comes through of something so

fine and so fathomlessly subtle and ever-radiant
it floods all available corners and

crevices with articulate information of the
kind you'd find in ancient theological

treatises carefully hand lettered on vellum
by long-dead cassocked devotees

whose immortality albeit anonymous

is rest assured by the fineness of their devotion
and the pure gyroscopes of their

sensibilities now encased in leathern
bindings as highly soaring over

prehistoric skies as pterodactyls
making a silent swoop and looking out

beady silver eyes at infinite pastures
filled with light that never stops

stuttering its God-pulsed exclamations
reflecting God's Self-referential and

never-ending Glory

                1/15

TWIG-LIKE BIRD PRINTS

One by one the friends drop away
and the enemies too

In an open prairie a cow stops to
contemplate her shadow

and plods on

One tree finds safety standing behind another
while saplings bare their bare barks

to the sun

Night stretches out both edges of
day in this galaxy

and the same by the looks of it
in all the galaxies that are

but only God knows for sure
Whose source of Light is

His alone spread in commanded increments
throughout the skies

making dazzling configurations
and appearing in all their effulgence

in the hearts of those of us
who've been so heavenly bestowed

and from whose fingers and faces some of that
effulgence pours

One person leaves the room
and ten more enter

Ten leave the room
and never come back

yet the room is never empty

How many hard surfaces do we
encounter in a lifetime

and how many soft beds do we think
we'd like to stay in forever?

But these are winter thoughts
as easily dispersed as a

change in the weather
out the same door

they came in
trailing clouds of glory behind them

leaving a patter of twig-like bird prints
in the snow

1/22

NIGERIAN SONG BIRD

The saddest song you ever heard
sung by a certain Nigerian bird

I never saw but he'd start at night
and his song would begin a flickering light

barely audible a kind of hollow crooning
already in a low octave then ballooning

downward in scale like someone weeping
and you wondered if anyone else was sleeping

or listening to this endlessly woeful lament
attracting some pitying mate meant

to assuage the bird's deep sorrow perhaps
but he'd continue all night his song collapsing

always downward downward ever downward
but I'll never know exactly which bird I heard

though it's in my head as I record it here
the saddest song you could ever hear

invisible in the dark
somewhere in Nigeria

1/25

(Note: A Kenyan man I spoke to said, even before I'd quite finished imitating the downscale: *an owl!* Often completely white and huge, and that if it flies into your house it means someone in your family is going to die.)

HE COMES RUNNING

The smoke from the camps rises up
and writes "MERCY" above us

and He comes running

In desert midnight a saint sees a star
with God's Face in it

and He comes running

In the sweet minutiae of our lives when we
pay attention the way a

squirrel in the snow holds
a crumb it's found

He comes running

In the wasteland of our hearts
low to the ground under moonless sky

He comes running

In the cry of a woman in childbirth
or a last cry of recognition on death bed

He comes running

It's in the very mesh and mechanism of our
ligaments and blood

written in the constant metamorphosis of
one event into another

kangeroos stampeding their shadows against trees
as wild fires crackle

as an unwary hunter meets a tiger face to face
and yells *"Burdah!"*

He comes running without fail
in this seamless divinely soaked

universe we've been sent to to
recognize His actions in

and our running to meet Him in these moments
one or ten steps at a time

closes the gap we might otherwise feel
and pours light of multifarious

colors across space
from His dazzling Face

as He comes running

1/27

INDEX

A Drunk Kept Knocking   43
A Giant Stood Up   25
A Little House   16
An Elegy to Loss   33
Any Hippopotamus   20
Black Horse   30
Cap and Bells   110
Car Sticker   32
Deep Foreverland   155
Did You Know?   36
Don't Turn Away Just Yet   119
Eating Stars   127
Eternity   106
Everything is Auto-Suggestion   52
Everything That Can Be Said   122
He Comes Running   166
He Comes Running   59
He Waits by the Gate   158
His Voice   51
I Awaken Each Day   157
I Wonder   23
If a Beam of Light   15
If a Centipede   13
If We Could Step Inside   144
If We Put a Thousand Bridges   129
Joy in God's World   142
Miracle Inspection   27
Motionless Flashes in the Air   41

Myths We Never Knew   98
New Boots   153
Nigerian Song Bird   165
Our Hearts are Gongs   121
Prayer   31
Scritch Scratch   18
Sitting on Top of the Planet   138
Sitting With a Saint   151
Sphere of Light   140
Take a Bottle for Example   11
The Curse of a Moment   146
The Mournful Dog   39
The Rowers All Row   117
The Scent of the Lord   46
The Serpent That Sizzles   124
The Things   35
The UniverSoul Circus   113
There's Nothing to be Done   132
Time Holds its Breath   111
Twig-Like Bird Prints   163
Watching a Cat Drink Water   10
Well of Blue Water   134
Whenever Has God's Radiance   22
Wings of Oblivion   148
With the Sensibility of Gyroscopes   160
Your Whole Face   136

ABOUT THE AUTHOR

Born in 1940 in Oakland, California, Daniel Abdal-Hayy Moore had his first book of poems, *Dawn Visions*, published by Lawrence Ferlinghetti of City Lights Books, San Francisco, in 1964, and the second in 1972, *Burnt Heart/Ode to the War Dead*. He created and directed *The Floating Lotus Magic Opera Company* in Berkeley, California in the late 60s, and presented two major productions, *The Walls Are Running Blood*, and *Bliss Apocalypse*. He became a Sufi Muslim in 1970, performed the Hajj in 1972, and lived and traveled throughout Morocco, Spain, Algeria and Nigeria, landing in California and publishing *The Desert is the Only Way Out*, and *Chronicles of Akhira* in the early 80s (Zilzal Press). Residing in Philadelphia since 1990, in 1996 he published *The Ramadan Sonnets* (Jusoor/City Lights), and in 2002, *The Blind Beekeeper* (Jusoor/Syracuse University Press). He has been the major editor for a number of works, including *The Burdah* of Shaykh Busiri, translated by Hamza Yusuf, and the poetry of Palestinian poet, Mahmoud Darwish, translated by Munir Akash. He is also widely published on the worldwide web: *The American Muslim, DeenPort*, and his own website and poetry blog, among others: *www.danielmoorepoetry.com, www.ecstaticxchange.wordpress.com*. He has been poetry editor for *Seasons Journal, Islamica Magazine*, a 2010 translation by Munir Akash of *State of Siege*, by Mahmoud Darwish (Syracuse University Press), and *The Prayer of the Oppressed*, by Imam Muhammad Nasir al-Dar'i, translated by Hamza Yusuf. In 2011, 2012 and 2014 he was a winner of the Nazim Hikmet Prize for Poetry. In 2013 he won an American Book Award, and was listed among The 500 Most Influential Muslims for his poetry. *The Ecstatic Exchange Series* is bringing out the extensive body of his works of poetry (a complete list of published works on page 2).

POETIC WORKS by Daniel Abdal-Hayy Moore
Published and Unpublished

Dawn Visions (published by City Lights, 1964)
Burnt Heart/Ode to the War Dead (published by City Lights, 1972)
This Body of Black Light Gone Through the Diamond (printed by Fred Stone, Cambridge, Mass, 1965)
On The Streets at Night Alone (1965?)
All Hail the Surgical Lamp (1967)
States of Amazement (1970)

___

Abdallah Jones and the Disappearing-Dust Caper (published by The Ecstatic Exchange/Crescent Series, 2006)
'Ala ud-Deen and the Magic Lamp (published by The Ecstatic Exchange, 2011)
The Chronicles of Akhira (1981) (published by Zilzal Press with Typoglyphs by Karl Kempton, 1986; published in Sparrow on the Prophet's Tomb by The Ecstatic Exchange, 2009)
Mouloud (1984) (A Zilzal Press chapbook, 1995; published in Sparrow on the Prophet's Tomb by The Ecstatic Exchange, 2009)
The Crown of Creation (1984) (published by The Ecstatic Exchange, 2012)
The Look of the Lion (The Parabolas of Sight) (1984)
The Desert is the Only Way Out (completed 4/21/84) (Zilzal Press chapbook, 1985)
Atomic Dance (1984) (am here books, 1988)
Outlandish Tales (1984)
Awake as Never Before (12/26/84) (Zilzal Press chapbook, 1993)
Glorious Intervals (1/1/85) (Zilzal Press chapbook, ?)
Long Days on Earth/Book I (1/28 – 8/30/85)
Long Days on Earth/Book II (Hayy Ibn Yaqzan)
Long Days on Earth/Book III (1/22/86)
Long Days on Earth/Book IV (1986)
The Ramadan Sonnets (Long Days on Earth/Book V) (5/9 – 6/11/86) (published by Jusoor/City Lights Books, 1996) (republished as Ramadan Sonnets by The Ecstatic Exchange, 2005)
Long Days on Earth/Book VI (6-8/30/86)
Holograms (9/4/86 – 3/26/87)
History of the World (The Epic of Man's Survival) (4/7 – 6/18/87)
Exploratory Odes (6/25 – 10/18/87)

The Man at the End of the World (11/11 – 12/10/87)
The Perfect Orchestra (3/30 – 7/25/88)(published by The Ecstatic Exchange, 2009)
Fed from Underground Springs (7/30 – 11/23/88)
Ideas of the Heart (11/27/88 – 5/5/89)
New Poems (scattered poems, out of series, from 3/24 – 8/9/89)
Facing Mecca (5/16 – 11/11/89)
A Maddening Disregard for the Passage of Time (11/17/89 – 5/20/90) (published by The Ecstatic Exchange, 2009)
The Heart Falls in Love with Visions of Perfection (6/15/90 – 6/2/91)
Like When You Wave at a Train and the Train Hoots Back at You (Farid's Book) (6/11 – 7/26/91) (published by The Ecstatic Exchange, 2008)
Orpheus Meets Morpheus (8/1/91– 3/14/92)
The Puzzle (3/21/92 – 8/17/93)(published by The Ecstatic Exchange, 2011)
The Greater Vehicle (10/17/93 – 4/30/94)
A Hundred Little 3-D Pictures (5/14/94 – 9/11/95) (published by The Ecstatic Exchange, 2013)
The Angel Broadcast (9/29 – 12/17/95)
Mecca/Medina Time-Warp (12/19/95 – 1/6/96) (published as a Zilzal Press chapbook, 1996)(published in Sparrow on the Prophet's Tomb, 2009)
Miracle Songs for the Millennium (1/20 – 10/16/96)(published by The Ecstatic Exchange, 2014)
The Blind Beekeeper (11/15/96 – 5/30/97) (published 2002 by Jusoor/Syracuse University Press)
Chants for the Beauty Feast (6/3 – 10/28/97)(published by The Ecstatic Exchange, 2011
You Open a Door and it's a Starry Night (10/29/97 – 5/23/98) (published by The Ecstatic Exchange, 2009)
Salt Prayers (5/29 – 10/24/98) (published by The Ecstatic Exchange, 2005)
Some (10/25/98 – 4/25/99)
Flight to Egypt (5/1 – 5/16/99)
I Imagine a Lion (5/21 – 11/15/99) (published by The Ecstatic Exchange, 2006)
Millennial Prognostications (11/25/99 – 2/2/2000) (published by the Ecstatic Exchange, 2009)
Shaking the Quicksilver Pool (2/4 – 10/8/2000) (published by The Ecstatic Exchange, 2009)
Blood Songs (10/9/2000 – 4/3/2001)(Published by The Ecstatic Exchange,

2012)

The Music Space (4/10 – 9/16/2001) (published by The Ecstatic Exchange, 2007)
Where Death Goes (9/20/2001 – 5/1/2002) (published by The Ecstatic Exchange, 2009)
The Flame of Transformation Turns to Light (99 Ghazals Written in English) (5/14 – 8/21/2002) (published by The Ecstatic Exchange, 2007)
Through Rose-Colored Glasses (7/22/2002 – 1/15/2003) (published by The Ecstatic Exchange, 2007)
Psalms for the Broken-Hearted (1/22 – 5/25/2003) (published by The Ecstatic Exchange, 2006)
Hoopoe's Argument (5/27 – 9/18/03)
Love is a Letter Burning in a High Wind (9/21 – 11/6/2003) (published by The Ecstatic Exchange, 2006)
Laughing Buddha/Weeping Sufi (11/7/2003 – 1/10/2004) (published by The Ecstatic Exchange, 2005)
Mars and Beyond (1/20 – 3/29/2004) (published by The Ecstatic Exchange, 2005)
Underwater Galaxies (4/5 – 7/21/2004) (published by The Ecstatic Exchange, 2007)
Cooked Oranges (7/23/2004 – 1/24/2005 (published by The Ecstatic Exchange, 2007)
Holiday from the Perfect Crime (1/25 – 6/11/2005)(published by The Ecstatic Exchange, 2011)
Stories Too Fiery to Sing Too Watery to Whisper (6/13 – 10/24/2005)
Coattails of the Saint (10/26/2005 – 5/10/2006) (published by The Ecstatic Exchange, 2006)
In the Realm of Neither (5/14/2006 – 11/12/06) (published by The Ecstatic Exchange, 2008)
Invention of the Wheel (11/13/06 – 6/10/07)(published by The Ecstatic Exchange, 2010)
The Sound of Geese Over the House (6/15 – 11/4/07)
The Fire Eater's Lunchbreak (11/11/07 – 5/19/2008) (published by The Ecstatic Exchange, 2008)
Sparks Off the Main Strike (5/24/2008 – 1/10/2009)(published by The Ecstatic Exchange, 2010)
Stretched Out on Amethysts (1/13 – 9/17/2009)(published by The Ecstatic

Exchange, 2010)
The Throne Perpendicular to All that is Horizontal (9/18/09 – 1/25/10)
In Constant Incandescence (2/10 – 8/13/10) (published by The Ecstatic Exchange, 2011)
The Caged Bear Spies the Angel (8/30/10 – 3/6/11)(published by The Ecstatic Exchange, 2010)
This Light Slants Upward (3/7 – 10/13/11)
Ramadan is Burnished Sunlight (part of This Light Slants Upward, published separately by The Ecstatic Exchange, 2011)
The Match That Becomes a Conflagration (10/14/11 – 5/9/12)
Down at the Deep End (5/10 – 8/3/12) (published by The Ecstatic Exchange, 2012)
Next Life (8/9/12 – 2/12/13) (published by The Ecstatic Exchange, 2013)
The Soul's Home (2/13 – 10/8/13) (published by The Ecstatic Exchange, 2014)
Eternity Shimmers & Time Holds its Breath (10/10/13 – 1/27/14) (published by The Ecstatic Exchange, 2014)
He Comes Running (part of Eternity Shimmers, published as an Ecstatic Exchange Chapbook, 2014)
The Sweet Enigma of it All (1/29 – 6/18/14)
Let Me See Diamonds Everywhere I Look (6/18/14 –)

www.ingramcontent.com/pod-product-compliance
Lightning Source LLC
Chambersburg PA
CBHW032047150426
43194CB00006B/449